A Life Well Lived,
A Death Well Met

Praise for *A Life Well Lived, A Death Well Met*

"A lovely collection of personal poetry and present-day parables by one who regularly bears witness to death with a sincere heart. A lyrical reminder that like birth, each death is unique. There is no one right way to meet living and dying. Only our own way."

        FRANK OSTASESKI, author of *The Five Invitations: Discovering What Death Can Teach Us About Living Fully*

"As a hospital chaplain and hospice volunteer coordinator for many years, I have worked with patients, as well as their families and the volunteers who join them, during their last days, weeks, and months. One of the truly outstanding features of Will's writing is that he has been there during those times, too. He has known the feelings, even heartbreak, of people on the verge of these life-changing and ending events, both from his own personal experience and as a hospice volunteer.

In his book of poetry and prose on aging, death and dying, Will has found a glorious, eloquent and elegant voice for capturing the most important questions and feelings, as well as in pointing the way to make peace with all that is happening. He offers ways to live fully in the questions as well as for each reader to find his or her own answers.

I am grateful to have this wonderful book of writings to share with patients and their families, as well as volunteers, especially as they seek to live in authenticity and embrace all they are meant to experience in these final days."

        SWAMI RANI FERREIRA, Hospital Chaplain

"Dying, being with the dying, and moving on after the death of a loved one are all a kind of trauma that we need to live through and heal from. Will Holsinger shares his experience in facing and transcending life's ultimate trauma in A Life Well Lived, A Death Well Met. He does this with grace and compassion, reaching out to each reader in a unique and special way. There is something in his words for all of us."

        CONNIE MARKOFF, MFCC

A Life Well Lived,
A Death Well Met

William Holsinger

A Life Well Lived, A Death Well Met

Copyright © 2018 by William Holsinger. All rights reserved.

No part of this book may be copied or reproduced by any means, electronic or mechanical, including photocopying, recording, or any information storage and retrieval system, without prior permission in writing by the publisher except for the use of brief quotations in a book review.

ISBN 978-1-7327424-0-6 (paperback)
ISBN 978-1-7327424-1-3 (ePub)
ISBN 978-1-7327424-2-0 (Kindle)

Edited by David Colin Carr, davidcolincarr.com

Book production by Jeff Brandenburg

Illustration Credits:
   Sam Colburn (1909–1993)
   Lis Russell, p. xii (*two men on bench*), p. 12 (*fabric textile*), and p. 94 (*candle*).

Photograph Credits:
   William Holsinger: pp. 6, 77, and 82
   Bob Doerr: p. 95 (*author's photograph*)
   Anonymous: pp. 28, 30, 33

Published by Penthanos Publishing

will@williamholsinger.com

williamholsinger.com

First printing: 2018

Printed in the United States of America   20180912

Dedication

To my father, Galen Wright ("Joe") Holsinger
whom I love very much

Contents

xi	Acknowledgements
1	Introduction
5	Who is Death? What is Death?
7	Beyond the Curtain of Light
9	Neptune's Passion
11	Death is our Teacher
13	fabric of our lives
14	Be with Me
15	The Choice
17	As I Age
19	Afraid of Dying
20	Winter Storm
21	Rock Garden
22	tonight
23	inexpressible
25	God/No-God
26	Another Way
27	Running With Death
29	Pine Box
31	Waterfall
32	a wonderful life
33	downstream
34	Final Witness
35	Unfinished Business
36	busy
37	Each New Day
38	Going Home
41	regrets
42	Don't Cry
43	Perspective
43	The Prime of Life
43	Wisdom
44	No More Pain
45	The Accident
48	Last Days

49	When?
50	I Want to Die When . . .
51	When Death Comes
52	When I Die
55	A Call from Mark
57	Susan
59	Who Am I?
60	Diagnosis
61	broken wings
62	Whispering
63	The Way
64	~~no logic~~
65	Dying has no Meaning for a Cat
66	Vigiling with my Cat
67	Cat Waiting for Death
68	Vimukta on his Death Bed
69	For Jean
70	Sitting Vigil with Barbara
73	Search or Claim
75	With Bill
76	In Between
78	Waiting
79	On Awakening
80	Sitting Hospice
81	Filled
83	Ocean of Longing
84	things that are not so
85	Watercress
86	oasis
87	When I Arrive
89	So Old . . .
90	Reflections on Friendship
93	God's Messengers
94	The Candle
95	About the Author

"I like to think of death as a handshake."

Acknowledgements

I've had a lifetime of family, friends, mentors, lesson givers (those people I was less than grateful for until I realized the true value they brought to my inner life), and those who have permitted me to spend time with them at the end stage of their lives. Each of them is responsible for the best thoughts, feelings, and words in these pages. Without the encouragement of Carina, my friend and lover, however, this book would not have been brought to print. She also introduced me to my editor, David Colin Carr, who helped to smooth the rough edges.

Introduction

DEATH AND I are old friends. I first met death when I drowned at the age of five and was accompanied to a curtain of light. Somehow, I understood that when it was my time I would pass through the curtain and become a part of a loving and eternal community. In the same moment, I watched from above as a lifeguard gave me CPR and knew it was not yet my time. I woke up coughing water out of my lungs.

I never mentioned the experience to anyone until, as an adult, I shared it with my father. "No," he corrected me, "I gave you CPR." I smiled, touched his arm lightly and said, "Don't you remember, the lifeguard pushed you aside." His eyes widened and his jaw dropped as he recalled the event. "Oh my, you're right, but how could you have known?"

As a teen, I sat with death a number of times. First as my maternal grandmother lay dying, then with a friend of my mother as he waited. These experiences, along with many others, have given me a perspective about death and life-after-death that nurtures and sustains me.

I sat at my mother's deathbed as she lay dying of cancer at age 63. I cried and told her it was okay to go. She passed that night. As I delivered my stillborn daughter two years later, I experienced the bittersweet anguish of a life that would not be lived, but was somehow comforted by what I knew lay ahead. I was present for my father's death rattle—and again later at the death of an older friend, alone in the world, whose cancer had returned.

At a daylong workshop about caring for the dying I realized at some profound level that I understood what was being talked about more than I could put into words. At the suggestion of the retreat leader I went through the training and certification process of a local hospice program. Since then I've sat hospice and vigiled with many people during their final days and months and hours.

With many, this involved listening as they recounted and relived their past, putting their life into perspective, perhaps sharing things they'd kept secret for most of their life. One night as I helped a friend pack to move in with his son for his last few months, he recounted the many VW bugs he had owned, his wandering life, his regrets and joys. As I took my leave, he stopped me. "I've never told anyone about this, but it feels good. Thank you."

I visited for months with a gentleman in his mid-nineties. He talked about his first wife, who died in her early twenties, sometimes singing the love songs he had sung to her. I mentioned this to his two adult children. "Oh, no," they said, "he's only been married once—to our mother!" I did the math. They were in their early sixties. He simply had never told them.

So what do I mean by "a life well lived and a death well met"? Many things, perhaps even some that you may think of that do not come so readily to my mind. Certainly, many of us hope to have lived well. And each of us hopes death will be gentle when it comes. I like to think that living well—in the sense of kindness, service, and generosity of spirit—prepares us for death, both ours and that of our loved ones. I also like to think that I will welcome the time of my passing if I have done my best to reconcile old wounds and conflicts. In contemplating this phrase, my attention becomes focused on my own mortality, on the imminence of my death regardless of my health, on what old conflicts may yet need to be healed.

A "life well lived" does not refer to our accomplishments, but rather to an attitude, a *joie de vivre*, an emotional oomph we bring to each breath, each step, each experience, each encounter. Every day is new and fresh.

This attitude can start at any time. For the terminally ill, this attitude calls them to live beyond, perhaps outside of, their physical confinement and pain. It calls them to see the joy to be found even within the boundaries of the day stretching out before them. In my experience, the man or woman destined to die tomorrow often finds more peace and joy in today than those of us who have a less definite expiration date.

Much of these writings predate my formal hospice service. At the time I wrote them I wasn't necessarily aware that they were about living and dying. Only later did I see it. Some are reflections on the individuals I've sat with. Some contemplate my own passing. In many I try to imagine what the other person feels as they age and realize tomorrow may not come.

It is my hope that, depending on your relationship to death and dying, you will find some comfort, inspiration, and kinship in these words, that you will see yourself, or your parent, or the friend you lost in them. May you have a life well lived and a death well met.

Who is Death? What is Death?

Who is death? What is death? Is death waiting for each of us, planning and pining for us, making room for us?

Is death truly indifferent to the time and manner of our coming, playing and cavorting in the eternal cosmos, then acting huffy and piqued as if our arrival at the threshold is a surprise and inconvenience?

Is death a person? With a personality, even if only a dark and droll personality? Maybe death is merely a doorman, like the one at the old St. Francis Hotel, dressed up in faux finery with antiquarian white gloves and top hat, holding the door for us, disdainful yet accepting of gratuities.

Perhaps death is the doorway like the new x-ray machines at the airport, scanning for signs of life as if "life" were an explosive that could level the hereafter, ready to reject our entrance at the faintest hint of trouble.

I like to think of death as a handshake.
Death is checking to see if our grip is sure.
But if it's limp and diffident, what then?
Me? I'll be checking death's grip.

Is death's grip honest, sincere, warm?
If not, I'll veer off and haunt the halls of mankind for an eon or two, waiting for death to finally mature and grow wise, confident of its place in the slipstream of eternity.

Then perhaps, when death greets me as an equal, with a steady, open gaze, maybe then I'll let death walk with me awhile, catch a glimpse of what is just out of death's reach on the other side of time.

Maybe then death will hunger after me and then, then ...
I'll wait for death on the far side of life.

Beyond the Curtain of Light

There is a place of light that nourishes the soul
Where the pulse is gentle, the curtain sheer

We will find the loved ones who went before us there,
waiting

As we approach the light, the world loses its pull
Still, some come to the edge and are sent back

This light is a gift of knowing
A gift of heart comfort and spirit repose

It is where our loved ones wait for us

Neptune's Passion

I love the sea, its bounty, its mystery. I love to stand at the edge of an ocean cliff as rain falls and the surf surges and recedes. I love stories of the sea. I grew up reading and reliving Jack London's Sea Wolf and Tales of the Fish Patrol, imagining myself the hero and villain by turns.

I've explored coastlines and bays in power and sail boats, in kayaks, and along nearby trails. I've been stranded on an island by an unexpected summer storm. I've launched out to sea hours before dawn, fishing lines cast out, cursing the sea lions as I hauled in yet another dismembered salmon head. I've watched killer whales hunting in packs, manta rays sunning themselves in still waters, and sat nervously as humpback whales stared at me just before diving under my pontoon boat.

As an adult with more years behind me than ahead, I have often retreated to the coast to reflect. Many times I've visited an old mariners' graveyard set back from a narrow country road to nowhere, on a knoll now shaded by trees, silent testimony to those who have lost their lives to the sea. Many of the graves are unmarked. Centuries of nameless, faceless loss. Stories that will never be told.

One day as I walked the beach, contemplating the sea, Neptune himself rose from the surf, blue-skinned, a beard of fine-as-silk kelp, trident in hand. His look was one part death, one part fury, one part mirth, and a hundred parts sadness. Crabs of all shapes, sizes, and hues scurried forward with him as he approached. I was speechless, held firmly by the sand. Seagulls flew high overhead, keeping their distance and their silence.

Neptune stopped at the edge of the spring tide, just beyond the reach of the straining foam. He planted his trident firmly in the sand, then reached into a pouch of old netting that hung by his side. He held out a parchment. *Odd*, I thought. It wasn't wet, but dry and brittle.

He opened the scroll and pointed it toward me. "Here," his voice coming from everywhere, filling the air and every space in between. "Here is a list of every mariner, every swimmer, every soul I have claimed since the rains first fell and the seas began." He rolled it out on the beach, longer and longer, until it extended beyond the horizon. "This list," he went on, "will never be as long as the number of fish men have taken from the sea."

"Rare though it may be that I come onto dry land," he continued, his head bowed, "I must tell someone of the sadness I feel at this timeless exchange before I burst with the ache and cause great harm." I just stared. *What in the hell is going on?* I thought. *Maybe it's just a flashback.* As if he'd heard me, Neptune continued. "No one visits this stretch of beach except you. Your love of the sea, your reverie called me."

Neptune looked up—directly into my eyes, pushing past my outward gaze—touching a part of me I didn't know existed. Somehow, it all came crashing in, a tsunami of knowing: the grains of sand on all of the beaches of the world were markers for the fish taken from the sea, each little pebble an untold story. The salt in the sea was Neptune's tears, a ceaseless weeping, waxing, and waning with the moon. It was a cycle of life and death that would never, ever end.

In exchange, seafarers, fishermen, all who risked the world of water, were taken—sometimes in a fit of rage, sometimes lowered to the depths as sacrifice, sometimes only reluctantly accepted. At other times they were thrown back to the shore, unscathed.

There was no bargain to be struck, no exchange to be made, no balance sheet to be tallied, no debt to be paid, nor scales to be tipped. Neptune would return to the sea, where he would forever cry salty tears for each dear creature taken from his loving embrace, the memory of them added to an ever-widening shore.

Death is our Teacher

Death makes the important things clear.

The important things are not world peace, an end to hunger and poverty, or other issues affecting billions of people.

The important things are the smile I'm sure I saw as you waited for me, the honey bee finding just the right flower, the butterfly just emerging.

Important things do not demand our attention, they wait to be discovered.

Important things do not change lives, they change a life.

The important things in life are the things we don't know are important until they're gone.

Yes, we have much to be grateful for, to praise and give thanks for ... if we're paying attention. But these are not the important things.

Rather, we are an important thing if someone else is thankful for something we have said or done. We are an important thing if someone else realizes how special we are after we have gone.

In this way, Death is a teacher.

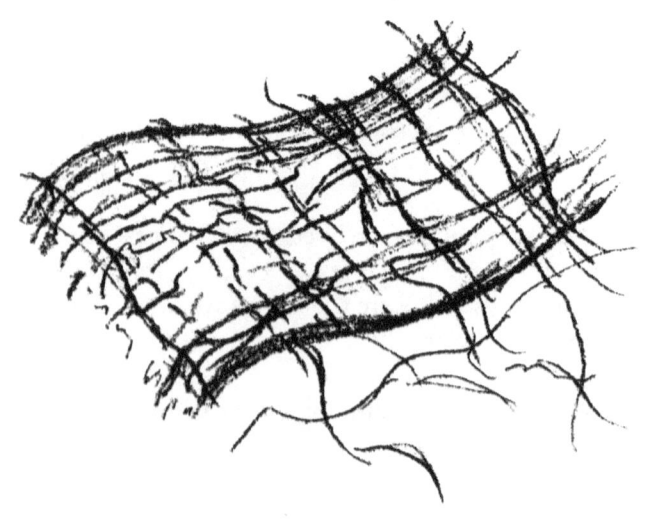

fabric of our lives

the fabric of our lives is a rich weave
soft silks, coarse hemp, layer upon layer
a tactile madhouse of no apparent design

the artisan knows better . . . the artisan sees a kaleidoscope
of beauty reflected within and without, a purpose
known to each of us if we but ask

and listen for the answer

Be with Me

Taste of my fear. It is a burnt offering
See into my reflection, where the light flickers
Dream my dreams. Forget them when the sun is high
Bathe in my pool. Only the undercurrent is cold
Do not waste the joy of discovery on old thoughts
Read my palm, all but the lifeline
Cherish simple hearts. Do not hoard time

The Choice

We speak and write from our experience, from our desires, and from our dreams. We cannot tell a story if we haven't lived it in our imagination, nor triumph where we can only imagine defeat. We retell and rewrite history as a means of creating our own future. When we do, our destiny collides with the history of others and the hopes and plans they have for their own future.

When we are busy talking or writing, we cannot see as God sees or hear as God hears. We are left to guess at truth. Nor can we truly know the dreams of others. We talk and write and talk and write until somehow, magically and for the first time, we glimpse something beyond our experience and imagination. We hear the voices of others who do not call but do not hide.

To listen more clearly, to see beyond our dreams, and to remove the limits of our own experience, we must become empty. We must become a vessel filled by the universe—emptied and refilled, then emptied and refilled time after time, moment after moment.

This then is the choice. We can hang on to our experiences, our desires, our dreams. Some may be worthy. Others will haunt us. Some desires will be fulfilled and some remain an unforgiving itch. Dreams will forever inspire and give hope that somehow it will all be different, be better.

The alternative is to reject the phantasm, step out of the mirror and into eternity, give up who we are in order to claim who we may truly become.

There is, of course, the middle way—the struggle to live in both worlds, to claim the rewards of an earthly kingdom and pretend we can move toward the light, then back. Progressing inch by inch, moment by moment. Then at the last, when we die, passing on through the curtain with ease and grace.

There is room enough for choice. There is less room to surrender fully and become an empty vessel. It is a demanding path.

We make our choice every day until the Choice is made for us.

As I Age

As I age, I become aware of the little ways my body protests and my mind rebels. As I go up stairs, I realize I am lifting each leg one at a time rather than simply walking up as I used to. Afternoons I find myself with my eyes half closed, resting for just a moment instead of planning an evening out, laughing and dancing little steps in anticipation. Now I look forward to visiting with friends of a weekend morning, rather than launching out on the trail at dawn looking for squirrels and the sun streaming through the trees, trying to work up a sweat.

It is not that I want to sleep, to escape my life, dream of exotic adventures. It is not that I want peace and quiet. It is not that I am complacent or bored. I will always rage against my own mediocrity and plot the next adventure. I will always be ambitious to do the things I did as a younger man.

Rather, I hear a call to prayer—and to quiet. I want to bathe in the slipstream of life, let it wash over me until I begin to swell, explode into countless points of light, each feeding the world and being fed by it. It is my cry to be ageless, to find a place beyond pain and fear, beyond sadness and despair, beyond loss. I ache to be joyous and free, unbounded by time or place or circumstance.

I will find, I will know, such a place. Just not today, just not now. Today I will experience all that life offers. New pains, old bones, new friends, old loves, those living and those long passed. Tomorrow, someday, I will have a tomorrow that calls me home. That will be the time, and only then, when I will remember getting old with fondness.

Afraid of Dying

After studying and meditating under the tutelage of his guru for many years, the student addressed his teacher:
"Forgive me, Master, I am afraid of dying."

The guru smiled, looking upon his student with patience and love, and replied:

"Then you have already died. All that remains now is how you will live."

Winter Storm

The angry sky blistered, all blackness, then
The crackling of white, yellow, and blue shards

In the distance a color show with drums
Nearer, the rain bit into the night as it glanced down

Sheet after sheet of lost sea returning home
Livestock shivering, wild things hiding in the shadows

I stood face up and challenged God, yet
The storm did not pause nor become personal

Even so, for a while I felt less small, triumphant
'til an oak tree lit violently and began its fire dance

As the death wind howled, I shivered,
Retreating into the shadows, no longer immortal

Rock Garden

I awoke, it was not time
To seek God or pray
I slept, it was not time
To dream or fly

I ate figs in the rose garden
Walked along the shore
Looked down, wept
Kicked at stones, cried out

When the tears dried
The moon waned
There were no more figs
I could not wake nor sleep

When the stones cried
Rose petals fell away
The rock garden crumbled
To dust

It was then
I met the traveler
Heard the music on the wind
Saw my reflection in the shadows

tonight

tonight I ponder ceremony,

death, and a firm hold

inexpressible

oh, to transcend, to live

to leap beyond the white fence

run without slowing, run and run

shinny up rainbows, shoo the birds away

dance from cloud to cloud, slide down sun rays

lighter than fairy wings on a windless day

fingers of a million comet tails

reaching past the stars . . . beyond

exploding with the joy of it all

God/No-God

Instead of pondering who is right and who is wrong regarding this God/No-God, religion, and afterlife business, I decided that everyone was right.

There is only one God and there is a pantheon of Gods. There is no God, no afterlife and no reason or purpose. We do ascend and return. There is karma. Vishnu is both preserver and destroyer.

Siddhartha Gautama's middle way is the best way. There is a purgatory. Christ was the only son of God. Birds and trees and valleys and rocks all have spirits.

There is room in heaven for only 144,000 Jehovah's Witnesses. There is only one prophet and Mohamed is his name. For those who believe, there is reincarnation.

Now that everyone is right, we all get to choose without fear that we are making the wrong choice. We can relax, stop the debate in our heads and with each other. We can have curiosity and respect for what others think and believe.

And we can change our mind anytime.

Another Way

The flatness of a passing night
Chalk dust strewn across an alley
Anger left bitter on a rocky shore

All these and more bind, but do not kill
Waiting on my decision to live or die
Or die then live. Damn!

Is it so hard to figure it out
To calculate the odds of survival, leave
The room before all Hell breaks loose?

I would not be cleansed, but only put on display
In a clear glass jar, waiting on a shelf
For inspection, salvation, chance

I must find another way

Running With Death
in Pamplona

First you see them coming
Seven tons of bone,
Muscle and horn

Six fighting bulls
Three steer guiding
All pushing their way
Through the crowds

Then you leap
Into their path, still
Three-quarters of a block away

Run! Run!

There is no escape
The pounding hooves
On cobblestone, near

All at once they are upon you
Death is upon you
With you
You with death, with the bulls

In an instant
The earth stops
Heartbeats go silent
No air, no wind

All silent.

No them, no me
No sky, no footfall

The briefest of moments
Expanding into eternity

And then . . . death is gone.

WILLIAM HOLSINGER

Pine Box

I traveled
upright
in a pine box
for days

just
to take
the measure
of the thing

Waterfall

I am a waterfall,
hidden by the wetness of time.
I stand at the rear,
holding back life itself.

The water bends angrily
as it washes over me,
anxious to hurry on its way
to a destiny far downstream.

As I stand or sit, fixed
firmly to this world,
I may guess at the wellspring
yet never know its birth.

I may imagine its journey
towards me, its softening flow downstream
yet never know the joy and sorrow
of arriving at the final destination.

I am fixed firmly in my purpose,
to keep the waters of life in check, upstream,
for the briefest of moments,
as it crashes over and past me.

I am a waterfall. I am more than enough.

a wonderful life

Firelight flies
beyond the edge
of knowingness
to the cliff
where resolve
falls away
the precipice leads
to an ancient tide
where caves hide desire
dreams lose passion

until the neap tide when
we escape
to a wider horizon of hope
beyond limits
beyond understanding
beyond life itself
to a place
where just being
is daily fare

none can know
or see
or feel
the fullness of this void
until the cup is passed
we've laid down our arms
surrendered to the joy that calls
our name
in the littlest of voices

bless you, bless you, bless you

downstream

We take so much for granted
There is no room for sorrow
This sadness that comes
When others do not see

I listen with only half an ear
The while I am across the hills
Plotting the course for
A tomorrow that never comes

Dream on, fool!
Burn an amber candle
Watch the flower drift
Away downstream, gently

WILLIAM HOLSINGER

Final Witness

Death stalks an unwilling dreamer
whose eyes close on the light
of reality. Not impatient or anxious,
we must all pass this way.

A portal to some, destination to others.
Whether or not chosen
We are rarely acknowledged
for this, the greatest challenge of life.

Death does not judge us, cares not
for the sacrifices we have made or
the pride we have stolen.
We are all, at the last, equals
in the eyes of this final witness

Unfinished Business

There is a whispering
In a far corner of my mind
A soft hum of passion
Just out of reach

When I pause and strain to hear
The little voices quiet
Waiting for me to be busy again
Moment to moment, distracted

I wonder at this dance
Wonder at the mysteries
I may never know, friends I may never have
The unfinished business of life

busy

we are all of us
rushing about
being busy, laboring,
when on passing
in the fog,
our oars brush
against
a sail-less mast
then drift away
to a distant shore
looking
for savages

Each New Day

Each day is grace
Mine to receive, but not own

Each day is blessed
I awaken to hope

Today is unique, alive
I will live it with intent

Days are not granted
without purpose

There is joy in this day
To seek it is the gift

I am alive at dawn this day
To honor my life, to live, thankful

Going Home

On awakening under the ancient oak, I had forgotten where I was, but somehow wasn't challenged to remember. The afternoon breeze was mild and the sun warm as I stood. I stepped out from under the shade of the majestic old tree. The path before me was well marked, seeming familiar. Instinctively, I turned eastward at the fork in the trail.

The silence was startling, as if the crickets had stopped and were waiting for me to pass before resuming their whirring and clicking. No birds called. The wind was muted as it moved through the brush and passed across open fields. I knew without thinking that the path would take me home. I saw tracks and sign left by animals, but none were to be found.

A darkness, transparent against the sky, passed overhead. The eagle soared by on its way to an unreachable aerie; a silent sentinel. Hunters such as these rarely utter a sound, only an occasional screech when calling to a mate, but even this was absent. This valley was its kingdom, the eagle was never challenged, yet . . . I continued east, over the rise.

A bevy of quail scurried about under nearby bushes. Ordinarily I would have heard the rustle of leaves and their soft cooing long before seeing them, but this was to be a noiseless trek. Neither did they appear to hear me. Mother and father quail kept their little ones naturally between them, not so much for protection as guiding them, always on alert. Quail are food for all predators, the eagle, fox, coyote, any who could catch the cautious little birds away from dense brush. For now, they were safe in this world without sound.

Approaching a clearing, I saw a small cabin on the far side, an inviting and welcome sight. As I stepped from the shade, the air was heavy and damp, a breeze at my back. Over my left shoulder, I noticed movement, a shadow just out of sight; it seemed almost to touch me, then disappeared into the wood, pausing just at the edge, waiting. Clouds formed without warning, heading eastward, too. I quickened my pace and pulled up the collar of my coat. I shivered.

The path ended at the front door of the little house. It was unlocked. I stepped inside. I stirred the ashes in the stone fireplace. A small tongue of flame rose up. I added kindling from a nearby box. Warmth reached out, into the room. The pine scent of the floor and walls was reassuring. I went to the sink, soundlessly filled a glass with clear spring water. It was good. Outside the clouds burst and rain began.

I sat on the side of the bed in the corner and reflected on my journey home. Where was the noise? No jays squawking in the oak tree, no crickets chirruping, all the birds strangely silent. The animals in the wood, usually so unafraid, at least of me, were evident only by their spoor. Only the shadow at the edge of the wood seemed alive.

I was unable to focus long on these mysteries. A great tiredness overcame me. I lay my head on the pillow and slept . . . again.

regrets

tarry here, my friend, delay
awhile as sounds alarm
and stories tell, push
outward on the slate grey
board with chalk in hand, intent
toward expressions mute
silence of soul, the day reveals
a mournful tone as bells
do sound abandoned notes
and pass this way, no more alone

WILLIAM HOLSINGER

Don't Cry

Don't cry little one
There is no place to put your lonely tears
Don't cry old man
There are no new days to reach beyond
Only heartache, no gentle words

Don't scream pretty one, no one hears
There is no place for you
Don't beg old woman, no one knows
No comfort nor family for you
Only dry and barren scorched dark earth, anew

The time is gone for hearth and home
The sun no longer turns
The brightness of new life is done
The ground is hard, yet yearns
For young new shoots to rise once more, anew

To reach beyond the cold and buried urn
To rise again and dream once more
That life will find its way back home
To a hearth that ever burns

Perspective

The Prime of Life

In his dream life, he came down from the mountain top, ate figs at the big house, drank from a shared cup, and danced with the moon. He only pretended to sleep, listening to the sounds of breathing all around.

He struggled to walk like the others, one step at a time, slowly, not knowing where each foot would come to rest.

Wisdom

The effort proved too much. He smiled sadly, turning full circle, arms opening upward, fingers spread. A deep breath, and his body shook mightily with relief.

Blinking slowly, he knew, finally, that he was not like the others. He came down from the mountain top, ate figs at the big house, drank from a shared cup, and danced with the moon. He no longer pretended to sleep, no longer struggled to walk like the others.

They welcomed him home.

No More Pain

The third breath
Was your last
Comforted
By a stranger
Not alone

The Accident

The wind was not so much strong, although the trees bent as it passed, as it was harsh. There was a bite to it. A fleeting thought suggested that every hard encounter, every angry glare and every word spoken with a hint of malice was in this wind.

I struggled to walk the miles home, my face into the wind and collar drawn up, wondering how I would explain the accident. It wasn't my fault, really—just one of those things. A cat ran out in front of me and I swerved, lost control, and found my car leaping across the ditch and into the tree.

We needed that car. We delivered hundreds of morning papers with it. It took us on our rounds to the rich folks' houses where we cleaned fingerprints off banisters curling upward and bathrooms that were rarely used. We needed the car for our annual trips home to see if my mom and dad were still alive. Sometimes, when work was slow, we needed the car to live in, parking in a different place each night so the police wouldn't bother us.

And now it was gone, one and a half tons of useless metal with a caved-in front end.

Miraculously, I didn't seem to be hurt, though I hadn't been wearing my seat belt. It hadn't worked in years, anyway. I gripped the steering wheel with both hands and rode that beast like a wild horse. My head came so close to the windshield that a few strands of hair stuck as I was whipped back.

My thoughts turned to my wife, at home in a converted one-stall stable in the back of the big house. We'd lived there for only a short while, but had been together three years. We weren't actually married, but it seemed as if we had been since we first met. I don't recall how it started, except she shared her re-heated soup with me one night at a homeless camp and we just sort of stayed together after that.

We had been invited to stay in the stable by an absentee owner who wanted it cleaned up in order to sell it. We had agreed to work 10 hours a week in place of rent, and had the remote property all to ourselves. The stable roof didn't leak, the walls were air-tight—more or less—and the door closed almost all the way.

After what seemed an eternity, I came to the lane leading off the road and turned into it. The long row of overgrown trees and the out-of-control hedge broke the wind. I felt a burst of unexpected energy and began running. Not a panicked running, not anxious or worried or eager. Just running, thankful I had survived and everything would be okay. I had been released. The car didn't matter. We would be alright.

She was waiting in the moonlight, silhouetted against the stable, an old shawl across her shoulders and her arms folded lightly against the night. A gust of wind blew across the front of the stable, a shadow passed at her feet and she shivered.

Last Days

There will always be the last days when we must leave. Sometimes reluctantly, sometimes eagerly, occasionally feeling harried. On these last days we look to the future if we are moving on or to the past with longing if we have lost something. We cling to the moment if it be our last. These are all last days. We must have them before we can have first days.

When?

When is it we will finally be able to sleep with a clear conscience, let go for that last 15 minutes, wake refreshed, rather than hurry, late to work or to walk the dog, to early morning Mass?

When is it we will finally be able to enjoy the local news, the sports section, and obituaries over a second cup of coffee, passing over world news of war, famine, and pestilence with a wry smile of knowing indulgence? "The young are so serious about everything."

Grandchildren get us there once in a while. The brief moments at the park when they run to us with excited smiles instead of tottering off in the direction of a busy street. They remind us of our own children and our many failings as parents, the missed opportunities and concerns over financial security—theirs and ours. (Wasn't there a time, not so long ago, when children simply took care of their aging parents because there was no other way?)

Just as I'm getting comfortable in my surroundings, the damn house needs paint or, for some inexplicable reason, I fall down on the way from the living room to the toilet and the next thing I know I'm in a hospital room with accusing eyes staring out at me from familiar faces as if I did something wrong. "Hell, I don't even know what happened!"

When is it I'll get to go home, get my driver's license back, be called for advice by that young shit that replaced me at work, and when will I remember where I left my glasses?

When it's my turn to relax, I just hope I'll realize it.

I Want to Die When . . .

I am afraid that I will die in the darkness of a soul less cherished by my sons and lovers, abandoned to my own small world of treasures gathered over a lifetime, then left behind without guardians appointed for another lifetime of selfish pleasure.

I am afraid that I will die in a corner, cowering with fear, in the pain of aloneness and doubt, gathering dust as I wait another hour, day, or world of minutes. In my nightmare, I die in a scenario I have selected carefully, without opening to the choices of others, not seeing their gifts of moments, no smiling or light or sound, no dreams, no gurgling of water rushing over rocks on a downhill run toward the sea.

What I truly want and pray for is to die when it is my time, when God is no longer tolerant of my requests for a stay of execution. I want to die at the end of a lifetime of service and joy and knowledge of the Great Friend.

I want to die after doubling back, confusing the trail and covering my tracks so that my presence will only have been noted by the touch of God in other people's lives.

I want to die when my pen is dry but the ink is still wet and the paper black with stories writ large and small across a broad canvas. I want to die when God says, "Enough, come home to Me," when He longs for my company in His house.

I want to die when I am so old and used up I am no longer able to make new friends, awaken to old ones, or step outside to greet the morning sun.

I want to die when there are no longer any first rains of the new season, when the floods don't recede, and when God no longer needs His willing servant in this world.

When Death Comes

Thank you, Mary Oliver

I want to know when it is the moment before I die, to taste the sweetness of clear water, feel the nourishment of the sun, and smile into the empty space between old things

In the moment before I die I want to remember the pang of longing, the ache of disappointment, and the joy that follows healing

When death comes I want to be home, with my bags packed, sitting by the fire, upright and ready, though not so long that I grow distracted nor so late so that I become impatient

I want to pause at the edge of the curtain of light, remember those still of the world, then press my palm against it and feel the rhythm of death

When it is over, I want to say . . . that it's all been said. I want the wonder and awe of the end and the joy of a new beginning to join for the briefest of moments as worlds collapse and there is no now or then or yet

When death comes, the dawn will be within my grasp

WILLIAM HOLSINGER

When I Die

When I die, I'll miss my children the most, those aggravating, whiny, sniveling little monsters, always needing, fussing, fighting, begging, screaming, crying real and imagined tears.

Their dirty diapers were changed by a heart filled with happy surprise at their unexpected little squirts, red faces, and unfinished business.

And what of the food scraps covering kitchen floors, spread on walls and chairs, squished between pudgy fingers that have explored everywhere before finding their way unerringly into my eyes and mouth? Such never ending messes will be cleaned up by those far less grateful than I.

I'll miss being caught in the middle between grandparents and those conniving little thugs who got bigger and better presents each year from adults competing for their narcissistic attentions. I'll long for the time when, at last, I realized my primary purpose in life was to clothe them in the latest fashions and satisfy their insatiable appetites.

These happy memories are nothing, though, compared to countless hours behind the wheel chauffeuring them to and from school (because they couldn't walk a few blocks), to soccer games, music lessons, and catered birthday parties where Bozo the Clown blew up toy balloons with uncaring eyes.

I'll miss the awe and wonder I felt when they sped off into the night in their own car. Actually, I won't miss much about teenagers. Mostly because I know so very little about them. They were never around. And when they were, their sullen grace, non-committal shrugs, and resentful you-don't-know-anything glares filled me with more ecstasy than a parent deserves. It was small consolation when these overgrown children returned home after "endless summers," lost jobs, and failed marriages of their own.

I'll miss their cautious attempts at reconciliation as they became aware of their own mortality, fear of parenthood, carpools, and nine-to-five job. I laughed at their efforts to achieve an uneasy truce in the present buying wars for their own children's affections. I'll miss the worry in their eyes as I grow visibly older.

When I die, I'll miss my children the most, God help me, I will.

A Call from Mark

God, I feel so unsettled. I've known Mark has been breathing towards his last for a long time now. But to hear his voice say, "Hospice is coming Wednesday morning," then work so hard to talk around his feelings, even to go so far as to feed his old madness by finding fault with others rather than sit in his own fear, just to hang onto his old self a bit longer . . . Well, it just hurts.

Susan

What remains uninvaded?
This gnawing death
takes no prisoners,
gives no quarter, leaves
nothing to chance

Her sacrifices were not enough
for this hunger without pity,
even her friendships devoured
by the beast with no eyes to see
nor ears to hear the pain

Taken from this life
unwillingly, her last great burden
was the fear and need and
ache of a young heart
ever wondering what love is,

never seeing it was all around
sustaining beyond life,
beyond death, beyond knowing
This love is in every room and heart
that will yet remember her name

. . . Susan

Who Am I?

Who am I, first I ask,
as all manner of beast and traveler
pass overhead, this way and that,
armed, bearing gifts, bearing shrouds,
bearing glad tidings and bad

Who are you, you wonder, as you go by,
this way and that, searching, selling,
longing, buying, teaching.
Rarely do you give me a second thought,
unless, that is,
I have vexed and annoyed you,
slowed your journey

I am the beginning, the middle, and the end,
I am life and death by turns,
depending on the seasons and their moods.
I am unique and yet one of millions, billions,
endless others.
I am the one you passed over,
the one who yearns to travel with you
and to be left behind

I am detritus caught up
on the back of an ass,
I am the one who nourishes nations.
I am a speck of dirt,
a grain of sand
I am nobody
I am dispensable and of no account

I call the stars brethren
and I do not hide. God
made me so . . .

WILLIAM HOLSINGER

Diagnosis

He was sorry to be the one to bear the news,
dressed in an unstained white frock coat.
"Weeks, perhaps months," he said, "we can
never be sure. You understand."

There is no cure, no treatment, nothing
to put off the inevitable. "Oh, yes," he added,
"we can give you something for the pain."
There will be pain.

Family, friends? He says I will need them,
especially near the end. Insurance? I know
I should have had it. But I just started back
to work. There's always County General.

The doctor looks down and studies his hands,
turning them over one at a time, slowly,
looking for hangnails in the silence.
(Who am I to say anything.)

broken wings

A dark tunnel
slowly descends
sound muted
light absorbed
into a black hole
no surcease from
the emptiness
an eternity
lost in the pit
insatiable
without escape
sucked down
into the vortex
dampness rotting
drowning out life
from the wellspring
falling, falling
freefall, helpless
away from heaven
no longer home
to a willful heart
I can't endure
coal black silence
but can't let go
the fear unseen

on broken wings
I search for thee

Whispering

I hear the cry of a baby who cannot smell the nearness of
its mother's teat, the flutter of fins of a newborn sea turtle
scrambling for an ocean it has never known.
I hear the call of the baleen whale for its lost mate,
the silence of an owl as it searches out the vole to feed its brood.

I hear the call of eternity while I am yet on this side of time.
I know the wind as it seeks out its own heartbeat.
I hear the sigh of longing fulfilled, know the prize hidden within
the shroud.
I am that close and I am unafraid.

The Way

Where do you turn,

    what road do you follow

When there is no map

    to guide you?

Turn to the sun each morning,

    rest at mid-day,

Follow it to twilight.

    There is no surer way.

~~no logic~~

i saw a butterfly
struck by lightning
fall to earth
unsinged, but dead
(very dead)

i touched a whale carcass
rotting slowly in the heat
on desolate beach
no teeth marks, but dead
(very dead)

i rode in a fast car
painted driver
laughing, out of control
the cat had no chance
(but lived)

i caught her
as she came into this world
and did not cry
no chance
(why God?)

Dying has no Meaning for a Cat

Dying has no meaning for a cat
There is only Now. This moment
The cat surveys its world
It does not reflect on the past,
Live for the future

Until it is time to lick its paw,
The paw remains firmly in place
The cat does not raise its paw,
Examine it, contemplate it,
Compare it to other paws it has known

In perfect repose the cat waits, immutable

Even when pain comes there is no death
Only the pain, the expression of the pain
The cat does not seek escape
In another room, another place
The pain is its world

Dreams of freedom from pain
Are best left to other species, like Man
When Man expresses pain in the presence
Of a cat, the cat does not flee or seek
To comfort the Man

The cat sits
Life or death, it's all the same

Vigiling with my Cat

He waited all day at home, sleeping and resting on the bed and listening to jazz. On arriving home I see that his eyes are open, clear, his spirit at ease. He wants to sit on my lap and be near me.

He hasn't eaten in more than two days and barely drinks any water. He's thin, bony, can hardly stand. He hasn't groomed himself in over a week.

He is not confused or afraid or in pain.

I worked all day. Reading, typing, talking on the phone. Listening to Enya. On arriving home, I see he is still with us. My eyes fill with tears and concern, my spirit uncertain. I want him to sit on my lap and be near me, but know he cannot.

I eat and drink and am overweight and out of shape. I groom myself carefully every morning. I don't brush him anymore because he's too frail.

I am not confused or afraid, but my heart aches.

Cat Waiting for Death

My new cat, Robbie, is sitting quietly and waiting. I inherited him from my friend, Joan. She died two months ago. Robbie was with her for over 12 years.

Is Robbie immutable or simply settled and reconciled? Does he hear you, Joan? Feel your presence? Are you waiting for him? Robbie does not need me. But he does more than tolerate me. He is kind and patient and at ease. There is no struggle, or hunger, or thirst. I feel your presence through him, Joan, but only fleetingly, as the barest of tingles at the edge of my awareness. I feel Robbie more clearly. Perhaps that is because the specter and presence of death is more familiar to me than the essence of those who have already passed and drifted away. Still, there is an intactness to my sense of you. You remain a teacher. What I've learned is that death is death, no matter it comes to human or animal. It is still death. Not heavy and dark, but quiet and calm. Robbie has this wisdom. He learned it from you, Joan.

Vimukta on his Death Bed

His left knee was up, stiff
Angled in, then out as he turned
His mouth open, seemingly breathless
Waiting for his spirit to pass

Focusing outward was an effort, beyond him
He struggled to see there
Long forgotten was this life

Shades drawn
His only smile was for the touch of another
Also waiting

For Jean

When we peel away the distractions of today
Lay down the fears of tomorrow
When we deny Mother Earth, Father Sun, Water and Fire,
The seeds of destruction sown by others in our heart,
When we surrender to the call for joy within us all,
It is then we hear past the Sirens' call to the sweet sound of silence

Sitting Vigil with Barbara

Barbara was resting quietly when I arrived at 7:00 a.m. to relieve the night attendant the family had engaged. When her husband and daughter visited the day before, she was alert and spoke and drank water. This morning she is not present.

After ten minutes, Barbara roused a bit and looked at me. I introduced myself by first name and said I was a friend of her daughter. When I asked if she was thirsty, she gave the barest of nods. I placed the straw to her lips. She couldn't quite open her mouth, but was able to get all the water in the glass. I refilled it and brought it back to her. She had her fill and eased back.

Barbara is still a beautiful woman. She rests easily with a calm, even face, right shoulder tilted slightly down. Easy listening music plays on the TV music channel. The bed light is on and daylight is beginning to come into the room. The sound of a new day comes through the hall door.

As I sit, Barbara's mouth relaxes, drooping down on both sides. Her eyes stay shut without effort. I hear the creaking of the plastic sheet under her on the bed. The people in the photo collage on the wall seem to look down on her.

Barbara's mouth opens a bit and there is the faintest sound of breathing steadily in and out, as she seems focused on images, perhaps voices, in a dream, not too far away.

One of the staff arrives at 7:25 to give Barbara some pain drops. Barbara moans a bit and asks for water in a clear but weak voice. The aide applies lipstick and speaks to her in a lilting voice. She raises the safety bar back and leaves, greeting another resident in the hall on the way.

Barbara coughs lightly and settles in as the medication slowly provides some relief. After a few minutes, she wiggles the toes on her left foot, then stops, eyes still shut. She quiets into sleep.

At 7:50 a.m. the aide returns, this time with her husband, who also works here, to clean and change Barbara. He calls her "Mama." They explain what they are doing. There is no protest or discomfort. The reward is a sponge swab around the mouth and lips, a soft voice and gentle laugh. Finished just after 8:00, Barbara settles back in and the overhead light is extinguished. Gentle music comes again to the fore.

Clean and dressed, Barbara's face focuses, strains slightly, then softens. Her eyes open a bit. She squirms, as if readying herself to get out of bed, settles back down, eyes and mouth closed in a neutral expression.

After a few minutes Barbara moves her legs and twists her hips, a focused look on her face. As her body quiets and her face eases, it starts again. I wonder if there might be some discomfort, but it seems more to be a matter of focusing and imagining, then reconciling something. *Some sort of process?* I wonder.

Barbara rouses once more in obvious though not intense discomfort. "Do you have pain?" She nods. "Would you like something for the pain?" Her eyes open a bit. "Yes." I leave the room to notify staff. A nurse is called to room 114 over the PA system—several times. Barbara speaks. "I don't want to hurt." The nurse comes, administers pain drops and Barbara settles down, waiting for the relief. It comes.

8:30 a.m.

"Water. Water," she says. A sponge swab. She opens her mouth. More, she seems to say, as she opens and closes her mouth. Even after I give her more, her mouth stays slightly open. I offer a cup of water with a straw. She takes just a bit. Still some discomfort on her face. (Perhaps, I think, the pain drops leave an unpleasant taste.)

Again, "Help me."

"What is it?" I ask.

"Itching, my leg itches." I scratch gently, watching her face. I find a spot. Scratch and rub both legs. "My hip" she whispers. I find her left hip under the cover and scratch. Her face changes. Relief.

"Help me." I rub her face and forehead. Then her shoulder. Hold her hand. Some helps, some not. She settles and I sit down, watching. She quiets.

A power drill starts and stops down the hall. Voices rise from the dining room, just past the sound of the intermittent drill. A door somewhere squeaks on its hinges. I hear voices chatting, the drilling more insistent. Another door opens and closes.

Barbara drifts off.

8:45 a.m.

The soft sound of plastic under the sheet as Barbara moves. Just the start of a soft snore as she breathes. Her mouth closes, her lips purse. No sign of discomfort. She rests and breathes steadily.

9:00 a.m. All's quiet. My replacement arrives to sit vigil with Barbara.

Search or Claim

Do we guess at Mystery
Read tea leaves
Pray at a wooden altar
Fast and become light-headed, or

Do we knock impatiently
At the door, demanding admission
To a place beyond time
Queuing up for our seat on board

Do we wander the earth, seeking
A portal to the netherworld
A power place where worlds collide, and
The slipstream is warm

Or are we already there
Our only need to shed another layer
Shake off the dust of expectation, and
Arouse ourselves from a heavy sleep

With Bill

Waiting my turn to sit silent
with Bill.

He is waiting too,
but not for me.

Bill is waiting
for the path to be clear,
the light to be bright,
the curtain to be opened wide,
to be called home.

I am merely a companion
for the briefest of moments, perhaps
witness to the everyday miracle
of passing.

In Between

On death we dwell too much
Seeking lessons too late learned
Wrestling with souls beyond salvation
Caught up in the darkness

Does the light dull our senses
So much we cannot abide in sweet silence?
A warming glow is no challenge
To a people at odds with the ordinary

Black and white, up or down
Sweet purity or a blackguard's cold heart?
In all and in truth, where is
The solicitude of the soft unspoken word?

When God yields to temptation by
revealing Himself directly to us,

He tasks us to live without the solace
of awe at His lesser mysteries.

Waiting

A warrior's bone-deep ache
Is a night alone
Surrounded by emptiness
Death leaves a chill
Yet does not hold fast

The pit rises from my feet
I crouch to feel the fear
A toneless bell echoes
Until it rails at the impenetrable fog
Just out of reach

I know pain, but it
Eludes me, denies me
The solace of hope for healing
These days are long
God waits for me to be done

On Awakening

Each day these new beginnings
Die to an ever-widening history
Lost to expectations fed on little steps
Become larger by fear of mediocrity

Arthritic arms embrace nothing
Strength sapped by pain and regret—
Though the body be a cruel jailer
The mind is yet an Isle of Elba

But for love of my own children
I would feed on flesh of the innocent
Worship at a wooden altar,
Bathe in the fiery afterglow

Turning slowly, no color, light, or sound
I wait out the passage of time
Neither hope nor dread nor passion
To advance the dawn or slow the loss of innocence

Sitting Hospice

I sat guard as the young man lay sleeping, then lowered my own eyelids, waiting. His mother entered the room and thought to wake him, so that he might tend to his not-so-watchful company. I demurred as she suggested I was tired, claiming my role as silent witness and companion.

She stayed, talking of home far away, her many broken bones, the prescribed nasal spray she used daily, and the miracle that followed. She spoke of religion and blood and her son's needed surgery. After a time he roused and snorted, then returned to his somnolent state as we quieted, repeating this often enough to provide an occasional distraction. His mother chattered on, glad of the company and respite from her own vigilance.

Finally he woke and saw me, asked how long I had been there. *Oh, I don't know, what time is it?* "Five o'clock," he replied. *An hour*, I said. His face fell in disappointment as he realized there would be no reading today, but perked up when I suggested coming back on Friday. "Yes, please," he said.

Filled

What is this hunger
that consumes
but has no edge
spices our lives
but does not burn
leaves us yearning
and expectant
without fear or dread

This hunger is an ache
that rejoices in the call
for more, but is not
impatient, demanding,
petulant

It is the hunger
that does not die
lends sweetness
to the heart
and fires our eyes
satisfies the longing
for completion today
no thought of loss tomorrow
when sadly, gratefully
our prayers are answered—

even more
in our final repose
we know we have been filled
to overflowing

Ocean of Longing

A great longing, like the sea
Seeking the shore, wave after wave
Reaching out to the sand
Thrown back to the deep, again and again

I fasten on a rocky shoal, on
An endless stretch of coast
Grasping; kelp clinging to the shallows
(without the anchor rock, I drift away)

There is no joy, no freedom in this
Need outside myself. I am separate,
Apart, incomplete, awash and unbound
An ocean of longing

things that are not so
you're still gone

this morning you were not there, as friend
i arose and fled the day, again
until the clouds wrung dry the day
and i did not know why

tonight the young came home to rest
older not by much, but then
i did not see the pain and light
that graced the sky where they burned bright

tomorrow brings new threat of life
another morn, another night
the bread is risen, unleavened No!
these are the things that are not so

Watercress

I was eating watercress from the stream behind the house, tiny green fronds on soft baby stalks. It made my stomach knot up in little ways, a distraction from my mother's mock-stern look as I reached my arms around my middle and whimpered. The smell of hot apple pie was distracting, but I held my ground. She opened her arms and beckoned me to her, a smile of feigned resignation writ large across her faintly lined face. She sat me down at the kitchen table, turned to the sink counter and pulled the still steaming pie to her as she opened the knife drawer. "Milk, please," I asked in the quietest, littlest voice I could muster. I didn't see the smile, though I knew it was there. "Okay, sweetheart, get it out," she replied.

This play was acted out in many different ways each Saturday afternoon. Some days it was a splinter and fresh baked chocolate chip cookies. Others it was a real bruise and honest-to-God homemade ice cream with ground up real vanilla beans.

Now my mother sits rocking in the old folks' home, smiling at every passerby—except me. When I walk up to her, she gets a puzzled look on her face, then asks, "David, is that you?" David was my father; he died 15 years ago. A merciful death, massive coronary in his sleep. He didn't even twitch, or so I suspect. The neighbors told us she just started screaming early that morning. I think it's what sent her over the edge, though she held on for eight more years before she gave up and slipped silently into the fog.

"No," I respond for the hundredth time, "it's John, your son. Remember me?" Her eyes glaze over, she pulls at the apron she always wears and opens her arms, inviting me down on my knees, and draws my head to her chest, crying gently. I'm sure she remembers the watercress.

oasis

i lie waiting, patient
bathed in cooling shade
wanderers rejoice at my nearness
old friends and strangers welcome
      from bended knee
see your reflection in mine
drink of me, hands cupped
in prayer and adoration
lie down beside me and rest
pausing for the night
sleep beside me on your journey
but do not stay

      the isolation is mine alone

When I Arrive

I do not eat, but only run
I dare not pray this night undone
I cannot dream the sleep of kings
But only bow to unclean things

I am unbent and not yet cowed
By headless knights abed in shrouds
I would delight in slow release
To a life of love and quiet peace

No more do I endure this pain
My hand pulled back from yellow flame
Could not I claim a home uncluttered
By tombs and graves of long dead others

The conflict ends, this road does die
This endless fall no more alive
Aloud we moan, silent we pray
When I arrive, God let me stay

So Old . . .

What is this thing that is
So old, the sap seeks out the sun on a warm day
So old, the stars blink in homage as they pass in the night sky
So old, the light of day is a shadow from the dawn of creation
So old, even God's memory is tested
Perhaps it is the way of time and not time,
Where every second is a universe
Perhaps it is the cry of an angel in ecstasy
When mercy finds its mark
For me it is personal
This thing that is so old, it is
The illusion of death

Reflections on Friendship

My hospice client passed on a Friday evening while I was out of town. He was surrounded by family and friends and was comfortable. I wrote this as homage to "sitting hospice" with a man who became my dear friend in the year or so I was with him.

I am one half of a whole
I witness while the other half
Slowly dies

In this partnership
In the act of serving as witness
I am complete

Sometimes I sit bedside
Sometimes we walk together,
Slowly

Our partnership is a journey
With a beginning
And an end

For me it starts with a request
"Would you be willing?"
"Yes," I respond, "I am."

And just so, it begins.
Sometimes I sit bedside
Sometimes we walk together

Until the end

When the end comes
I am almost never
There

Crisis comes,
Life's end nears
Then descends

Do I rejoice,
Weep at tragedy,
Just leave?

The partnership has ended
The journey is done
I am no longer one half of a whole

Sometimes I sit at home,
Numb for a time
Sometimes I pray

Where is the holy place
Where can I inter the ashes
From this no-longer burning flame?

These feelings,
These questions are a gift
I wish to give thanks

To the creator of this partnership

I yearn for a place to sit quiet
To return to the maker
The depth of my soul

Made whole for a time

God's Messengers

God's messengers ride a soft wind
Bringing hope as water to a thirsty man
No promises needed in the Promised Land
Gently led home by His guiding hand.

The Candle

unlit, the candle waits
burning, the candle lights
a small corner of the world
and slowly dies

About the Author

Born in San Francisco, William H. "Will" Holsinger grew up in Inverness, a small town in rural West Marin with a winter population of 400 and a summer population of 800. For a year he lived in Olema, which had a year-round population of 30, not counting the dairy cows. After graduating from an eighth grade class of 24 students at West Marin Elementary School, he moved to San Mateo County where he enrolled in Mills High School, with a student population of over 1,200. Will has lived in San Mateo ever since, except for his time away as an undergraduate at Sonoma State College, law school in San Francisco, and a year in Washington, D.C. as a staff assistant for the late Congressman Leo J. Ryan (Dem. 11th CD), who was killed in South America in 1978.

Will Holsinger is an attorney in private practice in the Bay Area and a direct care volunteer with Mission Hospice and Home Care in San Mateo.

www.ingramcontent.com/pod-product-compliance
Lightning Source LLC
Chambersburg PA
CBHW030332080526
44584CB00012B/824